THE AVENGERS

IRON MAN CAPTAIN AMERICA THOR

...UPER HEROES #1-3
...ITER: **PAUL TOBIN**
...NCILER: **RONAN CLIQUET**
...ER: **AMILTON SANTOS**
...ORIST: **SOTOCOLOR**
...TERER: **DAVE SHARPE**
...VER ARTISTS: **CLAYTON HENRY & GURU EFX**

...RON MAN: SUPERNOVA #1
...ITER: **PAUL TOBIN**
...TIST: **CRAIG ROUSSEAU**
...ORIST: **VERONICA GANDINI**
...TERER: **DAVE SHARPE**
...VER ARTISTS: **ED MCGUINNESS & CHRIS SOTOMAYOR**

...AILS OF THE PET AVENGERS #1
...ITERS: **CHRIS ELIOPOULOS, SCOTT GRAY, COLLEEN
...OOVER, JOE CARAMAGNA & BUDDY SCALERA**
...TISTS: **IG GUARA AND CHRIS SOTOMAYOR,
...URIHIRU, COLLEEN COOVER & CHRIS ELIOPOULOS**
...TERERS: **CHRIS ELIOPOULOS, DAVE SHARPE & COLLEEN COOVER**
...VER ARTISTS: **HUMBERTO RAMOS & CHRIS SOTOMAYOR**

...SISTANT EDITOR: **MICHAEL HORWITZ**
...TOR: **NATHAN COSBY**

...LLECTION EDITOR: **CORY LEVINE**
...TORIAL ASSISTANTS: **JAMES EMMETT & JOE HOCHSTEIN**
...ISTANT EDITOR: **ALEX STARBUCK**
...OCIATE EDITOR: **JOHN DENNING**
...TORS, SPECIAL PROJECTS: **JENNIFER GRÜNWALD & MARK D. BEAZLEY**
...NIOR EDITOR, SPECIAL PROJECTS: **JEFF YOUNGQUIST**
...NIOR VICE PRESIDENT OF SALES: **DAVID GABRIEL**

...TOR IN CHIEF: **JOE QUESADA**
...BLISHER: **DAN BUCKLEY**
...CU..VE PRODUCER: **ALAN FINE**

SUPER HEROES #1

WEEK AGO. AVENGERS MANSION, NEAR SON AVENUE AND FIFTY-NINTH STREET._

WE'RE GOING TO TELL EVERYONE THAT THEY **HAVE** TO BEHAVE OR WE'LL **BEAT THEM UP?**

THAT WE FIGHT ON THE SIDE OF THE **GOOD,** AND THEY'LL JUST HAVE TO **TRUST** US ON THAT?

STEVE ROGERS. CAPTAIN AMERICA._

NATASHA ROMANOFF. THE BLACK WIDOW._

SHOULD I **WAVE** AND **SMILE** AT THE SAME TIME?

IT **IS** A SLIPPERY SLOPE. I AGREE.

WE'LL HAVE TO CHOOSE OUR MISSIONS **WISELY,** WHICH IS WHY WE WON'T TAKE ANYTHING THAT **THREE OR MORE** MEMBERS ARE AGAINST.

YOU CAN DO SOMETHING **SOLO,** BUT **NOT** AS AN AVENGER.

CALM OWN, STEVEN. **ASKING,** NOT RITICIZING.

I DON'T **MIND** TELLING PEOPLE WHAT TO DO.

S.H.I.E.L.D. HEADQUARTERS. FOUR DAYS AGO.

NO. WE'RE *NOT* ASKING YOU TO FIGHT OUR BATTLES, *OR* FUND THE AVENGERS...WE JUST WANT YOU TO KNOW WHO WE ARE--

N.Y.P.D. HEADQUARTERS: 1 POLICE PLAZA.

--AND WHAT *WE* CAN DO FOR *YOU*, FOR *NEW YORK*, AND THE *WHOLE WORLD*. WE WANT TO ESTABLISH THE BEST WAYS TO CONTACT US--

FBI HEADQUARTERS: J. EDGAR HOOVER BUILDING. WASHINGTON, D.C.

--AND FOR WHAT REASONS WE SHALL OURSELVES TAKE THE FIELD OF *BATTLE*. WE AS *AVENGERS* SHALL BE BEHOLDEN TO *NONE*, ACCEPTING *NO* DOMINION SAVE THAT OF JUSTICE.

1600 PENNSYLVANIA AVENUE NW, WASHINGTON, D.C.: THE WHITE HOUSE.

DESPITE THIS, WE DO ASK SOMETHING FROM YOU IN RETURN.

FULL AND OPEN ACCESS TO *ANY* AND *ALL* FILES, CONFIDENTIAL DOCUMENTS, AND ANY GATHERED DATA THAT MIGHT HELP OUR COMMON CAUSE.

CIA HEADQUARTERS: McLEAN, VIRGINIA.

THE BOTTOM LINE IS...WE HOP THAT YOU AND YO ORGANIZATIONS W HELP US, AS WE HELP YOU.

IN CLOSING, I'D LIKE TO THANK THE REPRESENTATIVES FROM *DOCTORS WITHOU BORDERS, OXFAM, MERC CORPS, RED CROSS,* AN SO MANY OTHERS IN COMING TODAY.

WE CAN MAKE THI A BETTER WORLD. AN WE *WILL*

ONE DONUT LEFT! WHO **WANTS** IT?

HOW DO YOU THINK THIS IS GOING?

AS WELL AS CAN BE EXPECTED WHEN YOU DECIDE TO BE A POLICE FORCE OPERATING OUTSIDE OF NORMAL LEGAL RESTRAINTS.

I ASSUME THIS TALK IS PRACTICE FOR WHEN YOU AND TONY ADDRESS THE UNITED NATIONS.

IT IS. MOST OF THE ORGANIZATIONS WE'VE TALKED TO SO FAR ARE ON THE FENCE OF WHETHER OUR ACTIONS MIGHT BE CONSIDERED CRIMINAL.

I THINK THEY'RE LOOKING TO THE UNITED NATIONS TO TIP THE SCALES.

FENCES **AND** SCALES. YOU'RE MIXING METAPHORS.

WORSE. WE'RE MIXING **POLITICS** AND **JUSTICE.**

BOUND TO RUFFLE A FEW FEATHERS.

RICHARD RIDER: NOVA._

WELL, *THIS* ISN'T GOOD.

COSPLAY?

YOU'RE JUST *SPOILED* BECAUSE YOU'RE USED TO *REED RICHARDS'* COMPUTERS.

SUE STORM: THE INVISIBLE WOMAN._

NOT THE *COMPUTER.* THE *NEWS* SHOW.

YES

--ANOTHER REPORT OF A WELL-KNOWN STATUE SUDDENLY TAKING ON A NEW FORM... THE LITTLE MERMAID STATUE IN THE COPENHAGEN HARBOR AT LANGELINIE HAS GROWN EXTRA ARMS.

THIS, ALONG WITH *SCORES* OF OTHER INCIDENTS, COMES IN THE WAKE OF LAST NIGHT'S TRANSFORMATION OF AUGUSTE RODIN'S FAMOUS WORK, *THE THINKER,* WHICH HAS ACQUIRED SOME FORM OF CONCENTRIC BANDS EMANATING FROM ITS HEAD.

FIVE HOURS AGO._

--BREAKING NEWS REPORT. SHOCKING EVENTS FROM NEW YORK HARBOR, WHERE THE STATUE OF LIBERTY HAS FALLEN PREY TO THE RASH OF STATUE TRANSFORMATIONS SWEEPING THE GLOBE.

THE VISION._

IT APPEARS WE SHOULD *RETURN TO BASE.*

LIBERTY NOW HAS WINGS. ARE THEY A *HARBINGER* OF COMFORT, OR SOME FAR MORE *UNSETTLING* MESSAGE?

ONLY WHEN THE *ARCHITECT* OF--ZZT-- THESE RECENT CHANGES IN--ZZT--THE WORLD'S --ZZT--MOST FAMOUS--

THOR. NOVA. VISION. YOU'RE WITH ME.

NATASHA. YOU'RE STAYING. I NEED YOU TO--

DOING MY NAILS AND WAITING FOR A CALL ISN'T EXACTLY MY STYLE.

SEEMS MY MEMBERSHIP IN THE SECRET SISTERHOOD HASN'T DONE ME MUCH GOOD.

DON'T TAKE IT PERSONAL.

YOU'RE LEAVING THE ONLY NON-SUPER-POWERED MEMBER HOME. I GET THE MESSAGE.

OR MAYBE I TRUST YOU ENOUGH TO HANDLE ANY CRISIS THAT--

WHATEVER.

OH, NICE. MAYBE YOU DO NEED A BABYSITTER.

NO PROBLEM. WE GOT THIS.

RIGHT. STEVE... WE HAVE TO GO.

HIS ISN'T FANTASTIC UR. WE'RE EAM, NOT FAMILY--

HOW SOON DO YOU TWO NEED TO BE AT THE U.N.?

ONE HOUR. IF WE COULD BE WITH YOU--

VISION. GET THE COMMAND CENTER SET UP. I'LL BE THERE IN A MOMENT.

WE GO IN *HARD* AND WE PUT HIM DOWN.

WE GO IN... WHERE?

THAT'S THE PROBLEM. ANYONE HAVE *IDEAS* ON HOW TO *FIND* HIM?

IT IS POSSIBLE I COULD ASK THE *NORN*, THOUGH THEIR PRICE FOR KNOWLEDGE IS OFTEN *HIGH.*

THEN LET'S TRY LESS *LEGENDARY* MEANS FIRST. ANYTHING ELSE?

UHH. COULD WE TRY *CRAIGSLIST? FACEBOOK?*

OR...OH! DOES HE HAVE A *TWITTER?*

LET'S GO WITH A LESS...*SOCIAL* MEANS OF LOCATING MAGNETO.

SCANNING A COMPENDIUM OF DATA, I SUBMIT THAT IT MAY BE USEFUL TO INVESTIGATE A CERTAIN RENOVATED WARE- HOUSE THAT UNDERWENT LARGE-SCALE FORTIFICATION LAST YEAR, ACCORDING TO BILLS OF LADING FOR SUPPLIES DELIVERED TO THE LOCATION AND CONTRACTOR'S INVOICES.

THE BUILDING IS AT THE EPICENTER OF FREQUENT CUSTOMER COMPLAINTS FOR WIRELESS INTERNET SERVICE INTERRUPTIONS, SIGNIFYING ELECTROMAGNETIC UPSURGES IN THAT PROXIMITY SINCE THE CURRENT UNKNOWN OCCUPANTS TOOK RESIDENCE.

YEAH. WE COULD DO *THAT.* BUT I *STILL* WANT TO KNOW IF MAGNETO HAS A FACEBOOK.

LET'S *GO,* PEOPLE!

SERIOUSLY, IF MAGNETO *DOES* HAVE A FACEBOOK, THEN WE COULD CHECK HIS STATUS, AND IF IT SAYS, *"HAPPY"*...

THEN NOW WOULD BE A GOOD TIME TO KNOCK.

BUT IF IT SAYS, *"MANICALLY AND TYRANNICALLY ENRAGED,"* THEN WE'D KNOW *THAT* GOING IN.

NOVA, WE'RE ALL NERVOUS. IT'S *OKAY.*

SHUT UP.

I CAN'T GET OVER BEING *INVISIBLE.* IT'S LIKE...BEING IN *HIGH SCHOOL* AGAIN.

BUT HOW LONG ARE WE SUPPOSED TO-- *UMMP!*

QUIET. THAT'S THE *TOAD.*

GENTLEMEN, I'D SAY WE HAVE THE RIGHT PLACE.

...END

NO *PUSHING!*

TIN, TEXAS.

THESE PEOPLE, THIS IS UNBELIEVABLE.

NATASHA ROMANOFF: THE BLACK WIDOW.

CHOOSE ME!

SUE STORM: THE INVISIBLE WOMAN.

DOGS! OUR HOT #S! ONLY EN BUCKS 'ALL!

BATHROOM TICKETS! GET YOUR TICKETS! EIGHT DOLLARS! NO LINES!

I'M NOT SURE IF I'M MORE DISGUSTED BY THE *CROWD,* OR THE *VULTURES* PREYING ON THEM.

IRON MAN. SEE ANYTHING IN THE SKIES?

TONY STARK: IRON MAN.

NOTHING UNTOWARD UP HERE. ANY POTENTIAL PROBLEMS BELOW?

ONLY FOR MY NOSE.

SOME IDIOTS ARE BURNING INCENSE. THERE'S SMOKE ALL OVER.

OTHER THAN THAT...NATASHA HAS SPOTTED *VEIL, TIMESHADOW, THE THIN MAN, WYSPER,* AND *MAYBE* A COUPLE OTHERS IN THE CROWD, BUT THEY'RE BEHAVING SO FAR.

NOBODY WANTS TO MISS OUT ON AN OPPORTUNITY TO LAND THIS JOB.

CHOOSE ME

THERE *ISN'T* GOING TO BE ANY *JOB*.

OH, HAVE A LITTLE *FAITH*, SUSAN. YOU'LL BREAK THE *DELICATE* HEARTS OF THESE POOR *WRETCHED* IDIOTS.

hOOSE ME

DO THEY REALLY BELIEVE THAT *GALACTUS...* THE *GALACTUS...* WOULD PLACE A *CLASSIFIED AD* ON *MEGSLIST* SAYING THAT HE NEEDS A NEW *HERALD?*

THAT'S *ABSURD.*

AND YET, THE *SHEEP* COME. BECAUSE IF THE AD IS FOR *REAL*, THEY COULD GAIN *COSMIC POWERS*, TRAVEL THE *ENTIRE UNIVERSE* AND...HMMM...

DO YOU KNOW OF GALACTUS'S *RETIREMENT* PLAN? *401K?* DOES HIS INSURANCE PLAN INCLUDE *DENTAL?*

HUH?

ARE YOU TRYING TO BE *FUNNY?*

WHAT'S GOING ON *DOWN* THERE?

NATASHA IS *MOCKING* PEOPLE.

PIPE IT IN TO MY HELME™ BECAUSE IF *FIREL* IS GOING TO SHOW U VALIDATE THE AD, T IT SAID ON MEGSLIST EVERYTHING IS GOIN' GET *REAL CRAZY* H AND I COULD USE " *LAUGHS.*

DO WE HAVE A PLAN, OR SHOULD I JUST CONTINUE TO MAKE FUN OF THESE PEOPLE WHO ARE LITTLE DIFFERENT THAN CULTISTS WAITING IN THE DESERT FOR SPIDER-GODS TO DESCEND FROM THE HEAVENS?

ACCORDING TO THE AD, FIRELORD SHOULD BE SHOWING UP AT EXACTLY TWELVE NOON.

WHEN HE *DOESN'T,* WE'RE ON CROWD CONTROL. OR...IF HE SOMEHOW *DOES,* WE WATCH AND REACT.

WATCH AND REACT? THAT'S THE SAME PLAN AS BEING A *SITTING DUCK.*

I ADMIT I'VE HAD *BETTER* PLANS, BUT WE DIDN'T HAVE MUCH TIME TO PREPARE, AND NOW IT'S TOO LATE.

BE MY FRIEND ONCE I HAVE THE POWER COSMIC... ONLY TWENTY DOLLARS!

IT'S TWELVE NOON IN FIVE... FOUR...

...THREE... TWO...

...AND... ONE.

MAYBE THESE CRETINS WILL HO[LD] THEIR BREATH S[O] LONG THAT--

WE DID *EVENTUALLY* GET THE CROWDS TO DISPERSE.

AMAZING WHAT A FEW *WIDOW'S BITE* STINGS CAN DO TO THE *HERD ANIMALS.*

I'M STILL NOT SURE HOW *FIRELORD* GOT *PAST* ME. HE'S SUPPOSEDLY *FAST,* BUT MY SENSORS *SHOULD* HAVE PICKED HIM UP. AND AFTERWARDS, HE JUST... *VANISHED.*

SO, WHERE ARE WE ON THIS?

I'VE ALREADY SENT THOR OFF TO THE *LOUVRE.*

WITH GALACTUS'S DEMANDS OR *PRICELESS* OBJECTS, I'M SURE WE'LL SEE A SPIKE IN WORLDWIDE ROBBERIES.

THOR.

I'VE GOT THE *VISION* AT THE *METROPOLITAN,* AND *NOVA'S* EN ROUTE TO THE *MUSÉE D'ORSAY.*

GOOD. I'M OFF TO THE *UNITED NATIONS.*

WE NEED A *WORLDWIDE POLICE EFFORT* IF WE'RE GOING TO FIGHT AGAINST THIS ONCOMING CRIME WAVE.

BYE BYE.

NATASHA.

OH. SUE. HELLO.

SO...IT'S BECOMING CLEAR THAT THINGS AREN'T AS THEY SEEM.

OH. HOW DO YOU MEAN? DID YOU HEAR...?

THAT'S EXACTLY RIGHT. I DID HEAR.

I SEE. HOW MUCH DID YOU HEAR?

WELL...THE SAME AS YOU, I'D IMAGINE.

THE SAME AS... ME?

WHEN FIRELORD WAS *TALKING*, HIS *SPEECH PATTERNS* DIDN'T SYNC WITH HIS KNOWN APPEARANCES. IT SOUNDED *NOTHING* LIKE HIM.

FIRELORD? OH...YES. *FIRELORD*. OF COURSE.

I NOTED THE SPEECH ODDITIES AS WELL. IT SOUNDED MORE LIKE SOMEONE *PRETENDING* TO BE FIRELORD, AND FRANKLY *NOT* DOING A VERY GOOD JOB.

AND I'M NOT SURE *GALACTUS* OR *FIRELORD* ARE TOO CAUGHT UP WITH THOUGHTS OF *TAXES* OR *TIME CLOCKS*, SO WHY THE MENTIONS?

THERE'S *MORE*. I'VE BEEN EXAMINING THE RUBBLE FROM THE MONUMENT THAT FIRELORD DESTROYED, AND IT HAS TRACES OF *PENTRITE*.

PENTRITE? THE *EXPLOSIVE?* INTERESTING.

VERY INTERESTING. WHY WOULD *FIRELORD* NEED *PENTRITE* TO BLOW SOMETHING UP?

IRON MAN'S ANALYSIS LEADS ME TO BELIEVE THAT THE STATUE WAS DESTROYED BY A *PLANTED CHARGE*.

AND IF FIRELORD *WAS* AN IMPOSTER, IT COULD HELP EXPLAIN HOW HE WAS ABLE TO GET PAST YOUR *SENSORS*.

MAYBE HE TRAVELED BY AN ALTERNATE METHOD. SUE AND I WERE DISTRACTED BY THE *CROWD*.

WELL, LET'S DO SOME INVESTIGATING *NOW*.

I HATE IT WHEN THINGS G WHEN THINGS G PAST ME.

I JUST DEALT WITH THE *NINTH* ROBBERY ATTEMPT, SUE.

I'M FEELING LIKE A *HOCKEY GOALIE* HERE. ALL THESE WOULD-BE ROBBERS KEEP TAKING *SHOTS* AT THE *NET*, AND I'M JUST *KNOCKING* THEM ASIDE.

WELL...GOOD WORK, BUT THAT'S A *HORRIBLE* ANALOGY.

DOESN'T MATTER. NOBODY HERE SPEAKS *ENGLISH* ANYWAY. THEY DON'T *UNDERSTAND ME*, AND I DON'T UNDERSTAND *THEM*.

HAVE YOU *ACTIVATED* THE BUILT-IN *TRANSLATOR* IN YOUR COMMUNICATOR?

THE *WHAT?* WE *HAVE* THAT? *SINCE WHEN?*

WE HAVE *GOT* TO SIT THAT BOY *DOWN* AND *TEACH* HIM HOW TO BE AN *AVENGER.*

OR WE COULD KEEP HIM *DUMB.* BOYS ARE *CUTE* THAT WAY.

HOW ARE THINGS AT THE *LOUVRE?*

STILL QUIET.

THOR'S KEEPING *THUNDER* AND *LIGHTNING* IN THE SKIES... JUST TO LET PEOPLE KNOW HE'S *SERIOUS.*

MANNHEIM, GERMANY._

CAPTAIN AMERICA'S SPEARHEADING WORLDWIDE POLICE EFFORTS. MOST JEWELRY STORES ARE CLOSED FOR THE DAY. AND IMPORTANT GALLERIES AS WELL.

THE *VISION* IS KEEPING BUSY AT THE MET.

ALL IN ALL, AUTHORITIES WORLDWIDE ARE DOING A PASSABLE JOB OF KEEPING PEOPLE FROM *STEALING* THE WORLD'S PRICELESS TREASURES.

BUT OF COURSE THERE'S NO LAW STOPPING THEM FROM GIVING *THEIR OWN* TREASURES OVER TO GALACTUS.

THERE ARE SEVEN DROP-OFF POINTS, WORLDWIDE, WHERE ANYONE CAN PUT IN AN *APPLICATION*, AND *VALUABLES.*

AND THEN THEY SIMPLY *DISAPPEAR.*

JUST... *DISAPPEAR?* PROOF OF GALACTUS?

PROOF OF *SOMETHING.* GALACTUS ISN'T THE ONLY ONE WHO CAN PULL *DISAPPEARING ACTS.*

WELL, *THAT* WAS IMPRESSIVE. YOU'RE NOT ONLY *BEAUTIFUL*, BUT YOU--

WE'RE ON A *MISSION.* THIS *REALLY* ISN'T THE BEST TIME TO FLIRT WITH ME, MR. *BILLIONAIRE PLAYBOY* TONY STARK.

I WASN'T *FLIRTING.*

THAT'S WHAT *ALL* THE *BEST* FLIRTS SAY, AND I DON'T NEED *ANOTHER* AVENGER GETTING TONGUE-TIED WHEN I'M AROUND.

YOU MEAN *CAP?*

UHH. *NO.* I MEANT *NOVA.* WHAT DO *YOU* MEAN ABOUT *CAPTAIN AMERICA?*

NOTHING. I WAS JOKING.

SO...YOU THINK *NOVA'S* FLIRTING WITH YOU? HE SEEMS MORE THE *BLACK WIDOW* TYPE.

NOW I *KNOW* YOU'RE JOKING. NATASHA WOULD *EAT HIM ALIVE.*

YEAH...WELL, THAT'S WHAT BLACK WIDOWS DO.

AND THE BOY HAS TO LEARN *SOMETIME.* THERE'S NO BETTER WAY TO FIND OUT WHERE YOU *STAND* THAN TO PLAY--

--OUT OF YOUR LEAGUE.

ON MAN! DARE TO SPASS IN E LAIR OF ACTUS?

WHOA!

BEGONE!

I GUESS WE DID. BUT I DON'T FEEL TOO DARING RIGHT NOW, IF THAT HELPS ANYTHING.

SHOULD WE RUN?

WE SHOULD! BUT THAT'S NOT WHAT THE AVENGERS DO!

POUR IT ON HIM!

SUPER HEROES #3

MANHATTAN._

NATASHA ROMANOFF: THE BLACK WIDOW._

HEY. MY NAME IS *RIPLEY*, YOU CAN *BELIEVE* THAT OR *NOT*.

YOU WE' *NOT* INV' TO MY TA GOODB'

DON'T *BE* LIKE THAT. *YOU'RE* BEAUTIFUL. THE *DAY* IS BEAUTIFUL. LET'S BE BEAUTIFUL *TOGETHER*.

CORNY. AND I'M *NOT* ALONE.

YOU *SEEM* ALONE. I'M NOT SAYING YOU JUST TOLD A *FIB*, BUT I'M *LOOKING* AROUND, AND I'M *NOT* SEEING ANYONE ELSE.

EVIDENCE *CLEARLY* SUGGESTS YOU'RE ALONE.

BUT I WON'T GO INTO THAT.

TRUTH IS, MY FRIEND HAD TO RUN OFF TO DO AN ERRAND. HE'LL BE BACK.

MAYBE THAT'S TRUE. MAYBE *NOT*. BUT ANYONE WHO ABANDONS *YOUR* ANGELIC PRESENCE *HAS* TO BE A LITTLE *DENSE*.

ONLY CHILDREN AND AMATEURS ACCEPT THE INITIAL EVIDENCE.

ANYWAY... I'M CAROLINA ...SSARRO. I'M AN ARTIST.

I'M BEING BLACKMAILED. COULD YOU TWO HELP?

YOU'RE THE BLACK WIDOW, RIGHT?

NATASHA. AND THIS IS VICTOR, FOR NOW.

FOR NOW?

WE'RE DECIDING ON A NAME. HE WAS ORIGINALLY JUST THE VISION, BUT THAT MAKES IT SO HARD TO INTRODUCE HIM AT PARTIES.

BLACKMAIL IS A POLICE MATTER.

I AGREE. OR I WOULD AGREE IF MY BLACKMAILERS WEREN'T SUPER-POWERED. BUT THEY ARE.

ARE THEY NOW?

YEAH. THIS GUY NAMED DIAMONDHEAD, AND A MAN CALLED THE OWL.

I KNOW THE OWL, BUT NOT DIAMONDHEAD.

VICTOR, DO YOU HAVE THEM ON FILE?

PRESS

DAILY

DAILY B

YOU CAN'T DODGE ME ALL DAY!

ACTUALLY, I PROBABLY COULD. BUT I'M MOSTLY JUST SETTING YOU UP FOR MY FRIEND.

YOUR FRIEND? I'M SUPPOSED TO FALL FOR THAT? THERE AIN'T NOBODY HERE BUT YOU AN' ME!

WHY DO MEN ALWAYS THINK I'M LYING ABOUT NOT BEING ALONE? DO I LOOK LIKE THE KIND OF GIRL WHO'S LEFT ALONE?

GEEZ!

SUPPOSEDLY YOU CAN TURN DIAMOND-HARD? I'M THE REAL THING, AND IF YOU--

AAAIGGHH!

THERE IS LITTLE REASON FOR ME TO CHALLENGE YOUR EXTERIOR DENSITY. NOT WHEN I CAN PARTIALLY SOLIDIFY WITHIN YOUR--

YES? HELLO, NOVA.

REED RICHARDS?

TELL HIM I'M *BUSY* RIGHT NOW.

THE VISION AND I ARE ON A *BLACKMAIL* CASE. HERE, SPEAK WITH VICTOR.

YES. WE ARE SPEAKING WITH A SAMPLING OF THE BLACKMAIL VICTIMS, HOPING THEY WILL LEAD US TO THE BLACKMAILERS THEMSELVES.

NO. I'M AFRAID IT IS NOT SIMPLY A MATTER FOR THE POLICE.

THE BLACKMAILERS POSSESS *SUPERPOWERS.* FLIGHT, IN THE CASE OF THE OWL, AND THEN A BRUTAL INDIVIDUAL KNOWN AS *DIAMONDHEAD* HAS THE ABILITY--

DIAMONDHEAD? YOU'RE *FIGHTING* DIAMONDHEAD?

HE'S MY *VILLAIN!* I'VE FOUGHT HIM LIKE *FIFTY TIMES!*

DON'T ANYTHING COMING HELP

Iron Man: Supernova #1

MINUTES LATER...

WHICH WAY TO THE *APES?*

IRON MAN. I'M KATE MCMILLAN, THE DIRECTOR HERE.

HOWDY. I'M NOVA.

WHAT'S ALL THIS ABOUT?

TWO HOURS AGO, THE *RED GHOST* ESCAPED FROM HIS *STASIS CELL.*

HE'S *CERTAIN* TO COME HERE TO THIS *CONFINEMENT ZOO* FOR STRANGELY POWERED ANIMALS.

BECAUSE WE'RE HOLDING HIS *SUPER-APES* HERE?

EXACTLY. EVEN ON HIS OWN, THE *RED GHOST'S* ABILITY TO TURN *INTANGIBLE* MAKES HIM A *FORMIDABLE* OPPONENT.

BUT WHEN HE'S TEAMED WITH HIS *SUPER-APES* AND THEIR UNCANNY ABILITIES, HE'S VIRTUALLY *UNSTOPPABLE.*

I KNOW THAT *REED RICHARDS* DESIGNED YOUR DEFENSES, BUT EVEN *HE* COULDN'T FORESEE HAVING TO KEEP OUT AN *INTANGIBLE MAN.*

WHICH IS WHY I BROUGHT THIS PORTABLE *STASIS FIELD GENERATOR.* IT SHOULD TRAP EVEN THE *RED GHOST.*

FOLLOW ME, PLEASE.

HERE'S AN APE FOR THAT!

PAUL TOBIN WRITER CRAIG ROUSSEAU ARTIST VERONICA GANDINI COLORIST DAVE SHARPE LETTERER
ED MCGUINNESS & CHRIS SOTOMAYOR COVER DACOBY LUCCHABIAL PRODUCTION MICHAEL HORWITZ ASSISTANT EDITOR
NATHAN COSBY EDITOR JOE QUESADA EDITOR IN CHIEF DAN BUCKLEY PUBLISHER ALAN FINE EXECUTIVE PRODUCER

CANDY? I DON'T HAVE *THAT* LISTED IN MY INTERNAL FILES.

YOU CAN'T LEARN *EVERYTHING* FROM A COMPUTER. *SOMETIMES* YOU HAVE TO COME OUT OF YOUR *SHELL.*

ZZZZING!

OOO. I *REALLY* DIDN'T MEAN THAT TO BE RUDE...IT'S JUST THAT I'VE GOTTEN TO *KNOW* IGOR AND THE OTHERS. THEY'RE *EXTREMELY* INTELLIGENT.

HOW INTELLIGENT? LIKE... *DOG* LEVEL, OR *REALITY SHOW CONTESTANT,* OR EVEN *HUMAN*-LEVEL INTELLIGENCE?

LOW-LEVEL HUMAN, I'D SAY.

WE'VE BEEN DOING A LOT OF TESTS WITH THEM. *SOME* WITH MIKHLO AND PEOTR, BUT *MOSTLY* WITH IGOR. HE'S PROVEN THE MOST RECEPTIVE TO THIS NEW ENVIRONMENT.

WHILE *MIKHLO* AND *PEOTR* REMAIN PROBLEMATICALLY DEDICATED TO THEIR *OLD* LIFE... IGOR CONSISTENTLY CHOOSES *CANDY* OVER THE RED GHOST IN ASSOCIATION TESTS

OF COURSE, *WE HERE* LIKE TO THINK IGOR LIKES *US* MORE THAN THE *CANDY.*

THESE *ARE* PRETTY GOOD.

ARE ALL DEFENSES WORKING AT FULL CAPACITY?

IGOR STOPPED THE BRICKS, BUT WE'RE BEING OVERWHELMED *AGAIN!*

I *THINK* I'VE GOT AN *IDEA!* MIKHLO'S *STRONG*, BUT HE STILL NEEDS A PLACE TO STAND IN ORDER TO REALLY *USE* HIS STRENGTH!

SKRAAAKOOOW

GRAAARRRR!

AND HE NEEDS TO *BREATHE!*

OOOK!

SEE? *THIS* IS WHY YOU SHOULD *ALWAYS* SHAVE YOUR BACK!

GRARRRR!

OKAY, KONG. *MY* UNIFORM HAS *INTERNAL SUPPORT* SYSTEMS!

BUHH-LOOOOGE

BUT LET'S JUST SEE HOW LONG *YOU* CAN HOLD YOUR BREATH!

JUST YOU AND ME, IGOR.

IGOR! YOU'RE SUPPOSED TO FIGHT ON MY SIDE!

NOT ANYMORE, GHOST! HE'S WITH THE GOOD GUYS, NOW!

WELL, AT LEAST UNTIL THE CANDY RUNS OUT.

SO BE IT!

ZZEEEEENNNN

IGOR...LEAVE HIM ALONE! AS SOON AS MY STASIS GENERATOR IS CHARGED THE RED GHOST WILL BE AN EASY CATCH!

IT'S PEOTR THAT'S THE DANGER RIGHT NOW.

EEEGHH!

EEEKK!

SOGGY APE DELIVERY SERVICE!

WHO ORDERED THE GORILLA?

OOK

HOW'S IT GOING WITH THE ORANGUTAN?

HIS POWERS ARE TOO STRONG. CAN'T EVEN GET CLOSE UNLESS WE CAN FIND A WAY TO NEUTRALIZE HIS--

...THE END.

NO! YOU HAVE COST THESE LITTLE ONES THEIR *MOTHER*, I WILL *NOT* ALLOW YOU TO ALSO TAKE THEIR LIVES!

RRROOOOOAAAAARRR!

RUN, BEASTS! AND NEVER RETURN!

FAREWELL, LITTLE ONES.

Ma-raw!

ENOUGH! I CANNOT *RAISE* YOU. YOU ARE *DINOSAURS*, I AM A *SABRETOOTH TIGER*, AND WE-- WE--

Gamrr?

Dbrr?

ALL RIGHT. COME ON, YOU TWO. LET'S GO *HOME*.

KA-ZAR WILL THINK I'VE GONE *NUTS*.

PERHAPS *SOME* THINGS DO CHANGE IN THE SAVAGE LAND.

THE BEGINNIN

MARVEL COMICS PRESENTS MS. LION IN:
TERRIER ON THE HIGH SEAS

Story and Art by Colleen Coover

OFF THE COAST OF MEXICO.

MAY PARKER, YOUR LITTLE DOGGIE IS SO CLEVER!

THANK YOU! MS. LION, SHOW THE NICE LADY HOW YOU PLAY DEAD!

YIP!

GOOD DOG!

NOW THERE'S A SAD SIGHT.

A LAND-LUBBIN' LAP WARMER STROLLING THE DECKS OF MY SHIP!

LAP WARMER! I AM MY PERSON'S BODYGUARD AND FITNESS COACH.

HAW! YOU BARK AT THE MAILMAN AND GO FOR WALKIES!

NOW YOU'RE ON A CRUISE DOING TRICKS FOR BISCUITS, ONLY BECAUSE SHE DECIDED TO BRING YOU ALONG.

HMPH!

I EARN MY KEEP AND MY PERSON LOVES ME!

I'M NOT SOME SCAVENGER LIVING OFF OF TOURISTS' GARBAGE AND SCRAPS!

HAW HAW!

DECK E

...MIX THE STUFF IN WITH THE CHICKEN. I GOT THE SOUP AND DESSERTS.

THAT TAKES CARE OF EVERYTHING!

YOU'RE SURE THIS'LL ONLY MAKE THEM SICK? I DON'T WANT TO...*HURT* ANYONE.

RELAX, SLY! THIS GUNK WOULDN'T HARM A KITTEN!

...BUT WHILE THE WHOLE SHIP IS BUSY TOSSING THEIR COOKIES, IT'LL BE A CINCH FOR US TO BREAK INTO THE CASINO OFFICE AND **EMPTY THE STRONGBOX!**

...AND WHEN THE SHIP DOCKS TOMORROW IN ACAPULCO, YOU AND ME WILL QUIETLY SLIP AWAY INTO MEXICO.

HA HA! I CAN'T BELIEVE HOW **EASY** THIS JOB IS!

OUR **LOOT** AND **GETAWAY** IN ONE SWEET PACKAGE! ALL WE GOTTA DO IS **SERVE DINNER!**

HELP!

THE COOKS ARE *POISONING* THE PEOPLE'S DINNER! WE GOTTA **WARN** THEM!

POISON?!

SKA-THOOM!

NO! THE TELEPORT GENERATOR! IT'LL--

≶WHIMPER!≷

THEY'RE SO GONNA MAKE US PAY FOR THAT.

OWWW...

WH-WHAT... WHERE...?

RUF!

YOU INFERNAL BRUTE! HOW DARE YOU INVADE THIS SACRED PLACE AND ASSAULT MY PERSON?! WERE YOU NOT THE ROYAL BEAST I WOULD HAVE YOU FLOGGED!

AND NO, I WILL NOT PLAY "FETCH"!

≶SIGH≷

THE END

Prom Queen

A TAIL OF THE **PET AVENGERS** STARRING **LOCKHEED**

BUDDY SCALERA
WITH CHRIS ELIOPOULOS
WRITERS

CHRIS ELIOPOULOS
ARTIST

SOTOCOLOR'S C. GARCIA
ARTIST

NATHAN COSBY
EDITOR

JOE QUESADA
EDITOR IN CHIEF

DAN BUCKLEY
PUBLISHER

ALAN FINE
EXECUTIVE PRODUCER

OKAY, SENIORS, *LESS* TEXTING AND *MORE* DECORATING.

PROM STARTS IN LESS THAN *TWO HOURS*, AND THIS PLACE NEEDS TO LOOK *MAGICAL!*

AND YOUR PHONES DON'T HAVE AN *APP* FOR *THAT*.

IF ONLY... =SIGH=

I KNOW YOU *DIDN'T* WANT TO HELP SET UP, BUT I BROUGHT YOU A *PRESENT*.

A HOW TO DRAW DRAGONS BOOK.

DRAGONS-- *AWESOME!* I ADORE DRAGONS!

I KNOW. DRAGONS SEEM TO BE THE *ONLY* THING THAT BRINGS YOU OUT OF YOUR *SHELL*, LYDIA.

JUST TRY TO OPEN UP TO *OTHERS* LIKE YOU DO WITH DRAGONS, OKAY?

I'LL TRY, BUT PEOPLE ARE *MEAN* AND *CRUEL* AND DRAGONS ARE--

Tails of the Pet Avengers featuring REDWING
"Birds of a Different Feather"

JOE CARAMAGNA - WRITER
COLLEEN COOVER - ARTIST
NATHAN COSBY - EDITOR
JOE QUESADA - EDITOR-IN-CHIEF
DAN BUCKLEY - PUBLISHER
ALAN FINE - EXECUTIVE PRODUCER

CLINTON HILL, BROOKLYN, NY.

HEY, YOU!

YOU'RE REDWING, RIGHT? IT REALLY IS YOU!

DO I KNOW YOU?

MY BUDDIES'LL MOLT WHEN THEY HEAR ABOUT THIS!

NAME'S MELVIN. I'M YOUR BIGGEST FAN!

THAT'S...GREAT, BUT--

DO YOU REALLY KNOW CAPTAIN AMERICA?

YES, I KNOW HIM VER--

WHOA! I'D FLIP IF I EVEN MET CA

TERRI

NOW IF YOU'LL EXCUSE ME, I'M ON OFFICIAL DUT--

WRROOOMM!

...THAT IS, IF MY WINGS CAN KEEP UP!

UNFORTUNATELY, MOTORCYCLES DON'T GET TIRED--

WAIT A MINUTE! IS THAT--?

IT'S MELVIN!

HE'S GOING TO GET HIMSELF KILLED!

ACK! ACK!

GRAAA! GO AWAY, YOU CRAZY BIRD!

WOOOSH!

HUH?

ACK! ACK!

AAAHHHHHHH!

CHUNNK

FALAFEL HUT

NYPD

KRAACCH!

POLIC

HEY, REDWING, WAIT UP!

WOW, YOU REALLY GOT 'IM GOO--

LEAVE ME ALONE!

WH-WHAT DO YOU MEAN? WE'RE THE "FANTASTIC FOWL"

WE ARE NOT A TEAM!

YOU HAVE BEEN NOTHING BUT TROUBLE! YOUR DISTRACTIONS ALMOST CAUSED A JEWEL THIEF TO GET AWAY, AND YOU PUT YOURSELF IN DANGER!

YOU WOULD BE DEAD IF NOT FOR ME!

HANG ON A SEC, FLYBOY--

HE ALMOST GOT AWAY BECAUSE YOU DIDN'T LISTEN TO ME. IF NOT FOR ME, YOU WOULDN'T'VE GOTTEN THESE JEWELS BACK, AND--

--YOU WOULD HAVE FAILED THE FALCON.